DEEPER DATES FOR COUPLES

A
12-WEEK SERIES
TO HELP YOU
GROW CLOSER AND STRONGER

LISA MCKAY

Publishers Note

This publication is designed to provide accurate information with regards to the subject matter covered. It is sold with the understanding that the publisher is not providing psychological, financial, legal, or other professional services. Unless otherwise referenced, all statements and assertions in this book are solely personal opinions. The author does not assume any liability on the behalf of the purchaser or reader of these materials. If expert assistance or counseling is needed, the services of a competent professional should be sought.

All rights reserved. Except as permitted under the U.S. Copyright Act of 1976, no part of this publication may be reproduced, distributed, or transmitted in any form or by any means, or stored in a database or retrieval system, without the prior written permission of the publisher.

Copyright © Karinya Publishing 2017

Published in the United States Of America by Karinya Publishing

ISBN Paperback: 978-0-9854809-9-8

TABLE OF CONTENTS

DEEPER DATES

SIX MONTHS AFTER my husband, Mike, and I moved our young family to Vanuatu, I went out to dinner with several other women I had just met.

One of them asked me what I do, so I told her I was a psychologist, that I ran a website for couples in long distance relationships, and that I was in the middle of writing my next book.

"What's it about?" she asked.

"It's a series of weekly dates," I said. "I'm taking things I've learned from studying positive psychology and creating activities to help long distance couples find new and fun things to do, get to know one another better, and grow together in their relationship. It can be difficult to do all that you're in a long distance relationship."

My new friend leaned back her chair and laughed.

"It can be difficult to do all that in *any* relationship," she said.

Then she stopped laughing.

"When you rewrite that for couples who aren't in long distance relationships," she said, "you let me know."

I told her I would, but I didn't really expect that to happen. We'd only recently moved, and just after we arrived Vanuatu was devastated by a Category 5 cyclone. We had two little boys. Life felt very full.

But I've thought about her comment several times during the last two years, and the look on her face when she said it. The more couples I talk to about their relationships (and the longer I'm married myself) the more I become convinced that it's not just long distance couples who want to find new things to talk about and do together, and who yearn to feel closer and more connected to their partners.

So I've made time to rewrite that series for all couples, and I've selected 12 topics and activities that will help you:

- Get to know yourself and your partner better (yes, no matter how long you've been together);
- Learn to connect and communicate more effectively; and
- Have fun with each other.

Deeper Dates will help you explore and learn more about personal strengths, sense of humor, love languages, adventure-seeking, personality, and a number of other topics. Many of these dates also incorporate positive psychology exercises that have been demonstrated to improve happiness and wellbeing.

In other words, if you do this series you will likely be better off as individuals *and* as a couple.

From seeing how this process is helping couples in long distance relationships, I'm convinced that this book will give you a process and tools to deepen and strengthen *your* relationship—and laughter, good conversations, and fresh insights along the way. That's a lot to gain from a two-hour weekly investment.

I hope you'll join me on this journey.

All my best,

Lisa

FREQUENTLY ASKED QUESTIONS

Before we dive in, here are answers to some questions you may have, an overview, and a few tips to help you get the most out of this series.

What is Deeper Dates?

Deeper Dates is 12-week guide outlining a series of dates for couples at any stage in their relationship. It will help you learn new things about each other, have fun together, and grow closer and stronger.

Each week for the next 12 weeks we will focus on a different topic.

I will give you some background information (strictly interesting stuff). Then I'll tell you about your task for the week and share some questions you can use to kick off discussion during your weekly date.

How much time will this take?

It will usually take you a total of about 45 – 60 minutes to read the chapter and do your task for the week. As for how long you want to spend talking during your weekly date...? Well, that one's up to you.

Do I have to stick to the "chapter a week" schedule?

No, but if you can't manage a chapter a week for some reason try to figure out a regular schedule that will work (say, a chapter every two weeks) and stick to that.

It's OK to take a week off here or there in the middle of the series if you need to, but you're more likely to actually finish the series if you create a routine around it.

OVERVIEW

Here is a look at each topic in the series:

[Week 1] Name Your Strengths

What are your strengths? You have more strengths than you might think—probably more than you know. This week we begin the process of identifying your personal strengths and labeling them.

[Week 2] Explore Your Strengths

How do your strengths work together in your relationship? We use a questionnaire to explore your strengths profile in more detail. You share your signature strengths with each other and explore how those strengths complement each other and how they can cause friction.

[Week 3] Share Something Funny

How important is it for couples to find the same things funny? This week we explore sense of humor "compatibility" and look at when having a different sense of humor can cause big problems in a relationship.

[Week 4] Learn To Speak The Language Of Love

What is your love language? We use a questionnaire to identify your primary love language(s), identify your similarities and differences, and look at ways to speak different love languages well.

[Week 5] Go On An Adventure

Why is trying new things good for us? We will learn why trying new things can make us happier and is good for our relationships. You go on an adventure together and talk about how you embrace novelty and adventure in life.

[Week 6] Lit Pick For Two

We explore how you like to spend your free time, and how and why reading is good for you and your relationship. You both read the same book, story, or comic book, and talk it over.

[Week 7] Let's Get Personal(ity)

What is your personality? What is your partner's? We look at whether opposites really attract, and what the best formula is for a happy couple. You use a questionnaire to identify your personality type and discuss your profile.

[Week 8] Be Grateful For The Good

Did you know some call gratitude the world's most powerful habit? We look at how gratitude makes us happier and healthier. You practice a gratitude exercise and discuss how you experience gratitude in your life.

[Week 9] Create A Care Package

You learn about the fascinating origins of CARE packages and create a care package for your partner. You will talk about gift giving in your family, and how that has shaped your expectations and hopes around gifts and holidays now.

[Week 10] Treat Yourself

We learn about the benefits of savoring, and how positive emotions do more than just make us feel good. You treat yourself to something(s) you enjoy by designing a beautiful day out.

[Week 11] Give To Others

How does giving make us happier and healthier? We learn four surprising ways in which giving is good for us, and 22 good ways to give to others. You perform some random acts of kindness and discuss generosity.

[Week 12] Choose Your Own Adventure

We look at all we've covered in this series. You choose your favorite topic to delve deeper into, and talk together about the key things you've learned during this series.

HOW TO GET THE MOST OUT OF THIS SERIES

To get the most out of this series, you should...

Make sure you both have access to Deeper Dates

The best way to do this is to purchase two copies of this book, and we've kept the print price as low as reasonably possible to facilitate that.

If you each have your own copy, then you can review the chapter whenever it suits you during the week without having to pass the book back and forth, and you can make notes in the notes sections throughout the book. That way, your book will become your personal record.

However, if you're sharing a book or *don't* want to write in your copy, visit www.coupleconnectors.com/ddjournal to download a free PDF Journal you can print and use to record your answers. This free 35-page Journal contains all the exercises and discussion questions, with space to take plenty of notes.

Do this series in order

It's not absolutely critical you do the weeks in order. However, some of the discussions later on reference topics covered in previous weeks, and I've organized the series so that the more intense weeks are followed by more light-hearted fun.

Schedule your weekly "dates" in advance

If you can, designate a regular "date" time every week for the next 12 weeks (even if that's simply 'on the couch on Sunday night after the kids are in bed, with a glass of wine and some snacks.') That will give you time during the week to read the chapter and do your task.

Do your tasks and make notes as you go along

Most things that are worthwhile in life take some concentration, effort, or discipline. This is no different.

You *will* learn some helpful and interesting things and have some thought-provoking and lively discussions if you simply read through the book and ask each other the suggested questions. However, you will go a lot deeper and gain a lot more lasting value if you do the weekly tasks and make notes along the way.

Your weekly tasks will usually take you less than 45 minutes to complete, and to help you keep track of your thoughts, insights, and questions, I've included journal space throughout this book. You can also download a free Journal you can print and use at: www.coupleconnectors.com/ddjournal.

That's it, we're ready to get started. Let's dive into week one!

WEEK 1

Name Your Strengths

Strengths are ways of thinking and acting that come naturally, energize you, and help you feel happy, absorbed, and effective. You have more strengths than you might think—probably more than you know—and this week you will begin the process of identifying your personal strengths and labeling them.

HAS ANYONE EVER asked you what your strengths are? Probably. And chances are it was during an interview. Being asked about your strengths and your weaknesses during an interview is so common now it's almost cliché.

So, what did you say about your strengths the last time you were asked?

Did you talk about being organized, self-motivated, or analytical? Perhaps you said you were good at communicating. Whatever you said, you probably framed your answer around skills you suspected would help you perform well at the school or in the job you were applying for.

Well, this week we're going to think about strengths in more personal and practical terms.

We are going to kick off this series by thinking about talents and inclinations that help us "do life well," not just those that can help us perform well in a job or program.

HOW UNDERSTANDING YOUR STRENGTHS CAN IMPROVE YOUR RELATIONSHIP

'Strengths,' you might be wondering at this point. What do my strengths have to do with my love life?

Good question!

People who know and use their strengths tend to feel more energized, fulfilled, and engaged in life. This makes them more interesting, inspiring, and fun to be around. In other words, using your strengths will make you happier and also make you more attractive to your partner.

What else?

Well, when you understand your partner's strengths, you understand more about what makes them tick—what drives them, motivates them, and inspires them. This makes it easier to connect with them and to encourage and support them.

Finally, knowing your respective strengths makes it easier to understand and appreciate your differences rather than feel confused, upset, or threatened by them. Understanding strengths can make it easier to head off some conflicts in your relationship and solve others faster.

Our strengths, I really believe, can lead to our greatest successes in life and in love. But before we talk about that any more, let's look at what strengths actually are.

WHAT ARE STRENGTHS?

Strengths are those ways of thinking and acting that come naturally, energize you, and help you feel happy, absorbed, and effective.

Strengths are not things that you *want* to be better at; they are things you are *naturally good at*.

When you are using your strengths, you tend to feel more engaged, energetic and enthusiastic. When you are using a strength, or talking about a situation in which you used a strength, you might "come alive" and become more alert, excited, and expressive.

In fact, this sort of natural energy is a telltale sign when it comes to strengths. You might be good at public speaking, analyzing data, or counseling others. However, if that activity doesn't usually give you a boost or a little burst of energy, it is probably not a natural strength.

USING YOUR STRENGTHS IMPROVES YOUR LIFE

So, strengths are things you are *naturally good at*. And using your strengths helps you feel happy, absorbed, and effective. Exercising your strengths usually gives you energy and boosts your mood. Overall, it makes you happier.

And did you know that happiness is more than a feel-good outcome—a nice emotional reward?

We'll talk more in Week 10 about the science behind why this is. For now, I'll just give you the punch line: Over time, happiness and positive energy translates to feeling more curious and creative, being more relaxed and upbeat, and having better relationships.

Now that's a lovely-sounding theory, you skeptics might be thinking, *but is there really any research that backs this up?*

Yes, plenty.

Here is just one example: In one research study, participants in a "strengths" group were asked to identify their signature strengths and then consciously use these strengths over the course of a week.[1]

The results?

These participants (as compared to a control group who did not do the strengths-exercises) reported increased levels of happiness and markedly lowered depression not just that week, but three months and six months later as well.

This is a big call, but the existing research is clear—knowing and using your strengths will improve your life.

YOUR TASK THIS WEEK

It's much easier to intentionally play to your strengths in life when you can articulate *what they are.* That is why we are going to start this series by pinning down what your strengths actually *are*, and naming them.

There are questionnaires out there to help you identify strengths—in fact, you're going to complete one next week. *This* week, however, you're going think about your strengths yourself, before looking at labels and concepts others have come up with.

If you take the time to answer the questions below *before* you do the questionnaire next week, (and especially if you write down your answers) you'll end up with a better and broader picture of your strengths. And the more you know about your own strengths—the whole, glorious, colorful range of them, not just one or two—the better they will serve you.

Brainstorm Your Strengths

Answer these questions here or in your *Deeper Dates Journal.* (Last reminder on this front, you can download the printable PDF journal at www.coupleconnectors.com/ddjournal if you don't want to make notes directly into your book.)

If something comes to you, write it down even if it seems simple or small. We can have a hard time identifying our strengths precisely because they come so naturally to us (and also because we have a natural tendency to focus on our weaknesses).

1. What are you naturally good at? When do you consistently perform well?

_____
_____
_____
_____
_____

2. What are things or situations that make you feel excited, energetic, or enthused?

_____
_____
_____
_____
_____

3. When do you feel most absorbed and happy?

_____
_____
_____
_____
_____

4. When would your friends or partner say you "light up" when you are doing or talking about something?

_____
_____
_____
_____
_____

5. What are some things from your past about which you are most proud?

____

____

____

____

____

Label Your Strengths

All of the questions above were designed to help you identify your strengths.

For example, take the question about what you're most proud of. These things are probably the direct result of your strengths being at play. Harnessing your natural strengths tends to help you perform well in ways you feel good about.

Now, let's spend some time naming those strengths:

Look over all your answers and identify different situations, phenomena, or activities that you've pinpointed as strengths.

Ask yourself what is at the *core* of particular situations or phenomena, and label any strengths you can spot.

Below, I've shared some examples and two tips for how to get the most out of this task. Don't let it feel intimidating and overwhelming! The point of this is not to identify every strength you possess. It is simply to start the process of getting more familiar with a wide range of your strengths.

____

____

____

____

____

____

____

Tip #1: Have fun with this

Don't hesitate to make up a playful word or a phrase to describe a strength.

For example, I have a friend who is extremely good at reading subtle moods and sensing when someone is upset. She calls this strength "sonar" in reference to a dolphin's ability to locate objects underwater using only sound waves.

Tip #2: Think broadly

Here is another example. When I first did this exercise, I realized that one of my strengths is posting pithy updates on Facebook about my life and the antics of my lively little boys—Alex, my happy-go-lucky two-year-old, and Dominic, my (ahem, *spirited*) four-year-old. Here's a status update from a couple of months ago.

> I had a pair of conversations with my two boys this week that perfectly captures a core difference between them.
>
> ***
>
> This morning, Alex was up on a stool watching me make toast, when he pointed to something on the bench…
>
> Alex: "That's cheese."
>
> Me: "No, actually, that's butter."
>
> Alex (laughing happily): "Oh, BUTTER! Butter, butter, butter. Butter right there."
>
> ***
>
> Three days ago, Dominic was sitting on the bench watching me make toast when he pointed to the butter…
>
> Dominic: "Can I have some of that cheese?"
>
> Me: "That's not cheese, buddy, that's butter."
>
> Dominic (sudden anger flaring like a match strike): "NO! It's CHEESE!"
>
> Me: "Actually, it's butter."

> Dominic: "IT'S CHEESE!!!"
>
> Me: "Here is a piece. Taste it. It's definitely butter."
>
> Dominic (eats the big hunk of butter and fixes me with a steely glare): "It's def'n'ly CHEESE!"

Writing up these anecdotes really gives me a charge. It "lifts me," and I consistently get feedback that I'm good at it.

There are a number of labels I could have attached to this strength. One of the ones I settled on was "facebook funny."

If I dig down a little, what that means to me is that one of my strengths is humor writing—catching funny moments and pinning them down in text (or "redeeming" hard moments by seeing the humor in them later.)

It doesn't sound like a big thing, does it? Being "facebook funny" certainly isn't a strength I get to utilize all that often in an office.

The point is, however, the more we know about our natural strengths the more we can choose to tap into those strengths when appropriate and intentionally craft opportunities to use those strengths more.

DURING YOUR DATE

After you've both had a chance to read this chapter and do your task it's time for your date this week.

You can start the discussion anywhere you want—the point is for you to talk about your thoughts and reactions to this topic, and what you wrote down during "task time." Here are some questions you might want to use to get the ball rolling.

1. What are four of your strengths?
2. What is one strength you use a lot?
3. Did you learn anything new about yourself this week, or name anything as a strength that you'd never really considered a strength before?

4. What is a strength you'd like to use more often? How could you do that?
5. What are two of your partner's strengths (things that they do well, that seem to come naturally to them, or that "light them up" and give them energy)?

Looking forward...

Congratulations for completing Week 1! Next week we will be exploring strengths more deeply. As part of that, we'll complete a fascinating online questionnaire that will help you think about yourself (and your partner) from new angles.

WEEK 2

Explore Your Strengths

This week you will use an online survey to explore your strengths profile in more detail. You will share your signature strengths with each other and talk about how those strengths can complement each other in your relationship.

LAST WEEK WE began to look at your strengths—those ways of thinking and acting that come naturally, energize you, and make you feel happy, absorbed, or effective. When you are using your strengths, you tend to perform well in ways you feel good about.

This week, we're going to explore your strengths profile in more details. But first, here's a little more information about strengths.

A LITTLE MORE ABOUT STRENGTHS

Did you know that an increasing number of psychologists are devoting their career to studying strengths instead of mental illnesses? These psychologists are essentially focusing on what's *right* instead of what's *wrong.* This emerging field has come to be known as *positive psychology.*

One of the most prominent figures in positive psychology is Martin Seligman, and this week we're going to use Seligman's framework to look more closely at your personal strengths.

When Martin Seligman first became interested in studying strengths, he spent time studying different eras throughout history, and in different cultures around the world.

From all this historical and social research, Seligman distilled a list of six core "universal virtues" that have been highly valued across time and around the world. The virtues he identified are:

1. Wisdom/knowledge
2. Courage
3. Humanity
4. Justice
5. Temperance
6. Transcendence

In Seligman's framework, each of these virtues is associated with several "character strengths."

For example, the virtue of wisdom and knowledge is associated with the character strengths of curiosity, open-mindedness, and creativity.

Seligman identified 24 different character strengths associated with the universal virtues, and then he designed the *Values In Action (VIA) Survey Of Character Strengths* to measure them.[2]

Today, this survey has been used in hundreds of research studies and is the backbone of many positive psychology initiatives. It is often used by coaches and therapists to help people better understand their personal strengths and guide them towards activities that will improve their happiness and wellbeing.

Last week you spent some time naming your strengths. This week, you're going to use the *VIA Survey Of Character Strengths* to look at your strengths profile in more detail.

YOUR TASK THIS WEEK

Before your date this week, you need to take the survey and answer the questions below. Let's get started.

Take The Survey

There is a free version of the *Values In Action (VIA) Survey Of Character Strengths* online. It has 120 multiple-choice questions and takes about 15 minutes to complete.

1. Go to the website of the VIA Institute on Character at https://www.viacharacter.org/
2. Click "Take The Free Survey" and register (it's free).
3. Set aside 15 minutes and take the *VIA Survey of Character Strengths.*

After you complete the survey, the Institute will show you a personal profile, rank ordering your 24 strengths. Your top 5 strengths are considered your "signature strengths."

The Institute will also offer to sell you various, more in-depth reports on your strengths, in addition to your free profile.

Feel free to purchase a report if you're fascinated by this topic. However, you don't need to buy your report to gain insights from these results. You will gain a lot of benefit simply by exploring your free strengths profile and answering the questions in the "Dig Deeper" section below.

Dig Deeper

Now that you've completed the online questionnaire and have your strengths profile in hand, let's dig a little deeper.

First, look at your notes from last week. What strengths did you identify and name?

Now look at your results on the *VIA Survey of Character Strengths.*

Spend some time answering the following questions and making notes:

1. What are your top 5 "signature" strengths?

____
____
____
____
____

2. List at least one way each of your top 5 strengths is evident in your life. How do you use that strength? When do you tend to see it in action?

____
____
____
____
____

3. Which two of your top 8 strengths do you use most frequently?

____
____
____
____
____

4. Remember that using strengths tends to generate enthusiasm, energy, and engagement. Given this, do you generally agree with your results on this survey?

____
____
____
____
____

5. How do your results on this survey "match up" to the strengths you named last week?

____

____

____

____

____

6. Does the survey highlight any strength areas you *didn't* consider last week? Which ones?

____

____

____

____

____

DURING YOUR DATE

After you've both had a chance to take the *VIA Survey* and think through your results, it's date time. Grab some cheese, crackers, and a glass of wine (or whatever your date night pleasures are) and talk this over.

There is a lot you could talk about this week. Here are some questions to get you started.

About your own strengths

1. What are your top-five "signature" strengths?
2. Does anything about your results surprise you?
3. What is one strength you use a lot?
4. What is a strength you'd like to use more often? How could you do that?

About your partner's strengths

1. Do you agree with your partner's "signature" strengths, or would you have guessed that other strengths would show up more strongly in their profile?
2. What are ways that you see their signature strengths show up in your partner's life?

As a couple: About your strengths together

1. What are ways that you and your partner have different strengths?
2. How can these differences be complementary and help you in your relationship?
3. How might these differences cause friction?
4. Do you have any shared interests that tap into both of your signature strengths?

Looking forward...

Good work on completing Week 2. See you back here next week when we lighten things up a bit. We'll spend next week exploring whether it's for couples to have a similar sense of humor and share some things that make us laugh, so start getting ready to smile now.

WEEK 3

Share Something Funny

This week you will look at whether it's critical for couples to find the same things funny, and when having a different sense of humor can cause big problems in a relationship. You will share some things you find funny.

THE DAY MY eldest son turned three, he came to me near the end of his birthday party and lifted up his arms. When I picked him up, he snuggled into my neck and whispered sweetly in my ear...

"I just peed in the washing machine."

And he had.

I laughed. It was either that or cry. (I'm finding that parenting young children often presents me with that choice.)

So, what have you read, heard, or seen that's made you laugh recently?

This week we're all about smiles, laughs, and everything in between. Your task this week will be to find two or three things that you find funny and share them with your partner.

First, however, let's talk a little about humor and how important it really is for couples to find the same things funny.

HOW IMPORTANT IS IT FOR COUPLES TO SHARE A SENSE OF HUMOR?

It's nice when your partner shares your sense of humor and laughs at your jokes (and your email forwards,) but it's not crucial. Plenty of couples don't always find the same things funny and still have great relationships—they have fun together, communicate well, resolve conflict effectively, and find each other attractive.

When people say that they want to be with someone with a sense of humor, they don't necessarily mean someone who laughs at all the same things they do. They mean someone who has a positive attitude and is able to see good where others might tend to see the negative, complain, or feel overwhelmed.

So, if you usually laugh at your partner's "funnies," great!

If you don't, look at your date time this week as a chance to get to know your partner better and vice versa.

But before we get to your date this week, a word of caution...

It's not *necessarily* a problem if you don't share a sense of humor with your partner, but it *can* be. If you and your partner don't usually find the same things funny, stay alert for the following signs of serious incompatibility.

WHEN NOT HAVING A SIMILAR SENSE OF HUMOR CAN BE A PROBLEM

A shared sense of humor isn't essential to a relationship, but it *is* important to feel that your partner "gets you."

If your partner doesn't get your jokes, that is one thing.

If you feel like your partner doesn't get *you*, that is another, much more serious, issue.

Your love doesn't have to sit on the couch and laugh at *Saturday Night Live* with you. However, if they sigh and roll their eyes every time they see you watching *Saturday Night Live*, you could have a problem.

You *definitely* have a problem if your partner's sense of humor frequently makes you feel:

- Insecure
- Put down, judged, and/or devalued
- Patronized
- Excluded
- Offended

If you often feel like this when your partner is trying to be funny (or, incidentally, at other times) you should think very carefully about how compatible you truly are and whether you really want to be in a relationship with this person.

THE BOTTOM LINE ABOUT LOVE AND LAUGHING

Whether your relationship works well probably has less to do with whether you laugh at the same things than whether you:

- Communicate well
- Respect and affirm each other
- Find each other attractive
- Enjoy spending time together
- Resolve your differences effectively

If you don't share a sense of humor but you love being with your partner, take heart! Your relationship is probably on solid ground.

Over time, you may even find yourself laughing at more of the same things. Humor compatibility and shared jokes often develop organically over time.

YOUR TASK THIS WEEK

Your task this week is to find two or three things that you think are funny and share them with your partner. Not sure where to start? Here are some prompts that might help...

- Have you read (or written) any articles, posts, essays, or books lately that made you laugh? What about status updates on facebook?
- Seen any videos on YouTube?
- Watched anything on TV or at the movies?
- Listened to any funny clips or podcasts?
- Is there a website that often makes you smile?

____

____

____

____

____

DURING YOUR DATE

Share or discuss two or three things you find funny. If you've selected a longer article or post you might want to send it to your partner in advance so they can take time to read it.

It's sometimes very difficult to explain why we find something funny, so this can be a bit of a tricky topic to discuss (particularly if you two have a very different sense of humor.)

Don't try too hard to dissect your "shares." Just enjoy. If you and your partner have a similar sense of humor, that will be easy. And if you don't think your partner's shares are that funny, that's fine. Just take this as a chance to get to know them better—enjoy their finding humor in life.

And that said, here are some questions you might want to about.

1. What has made you laugh or smile this week?
2. Do you have any favorite humor-websites? If so, what are they?
3. Do your parents have a favorite story about something funny you did when you were little?
4. When has your partner has (intentionally or unintentionally) made you laugh?

A NOTE ABOUT WEEK 6

That's it—Week 3, done. Before you go, however, a quick note about Week 6.

Three weeks from now, the topic is *Lit Pick For Two.* Your task will be to choose a book for both of you to read and talk about. You'll get more details during Week 6, but I know not everyone reads at the speed of light.

If you'd like to get a jump on your reading, you can pick any book you'd both like to read and get started. If you've both been dying to find some time to read *Calvin And Hobbes,* go for it.

But in case you don't know where to start with choosing a book, take a look at the recommended book list in Chapter 6.

If you choose a book together now and start reading, you'll be way ahead of the game when Week 6 rolls around.

OK, see you back here next week. We'll be exploring how we speak and understand the language of love, and whether you and your partner tend to speak the *same* language. Did you know many couples *don't*?

WEEK 4

Learn To Speak The Language Of Love

This week you will use the love languages survey to identify your primary love language(s) and your similarities and differences. You will look at ways to speak different love languages effectively.

HAVE YOU EVER put time and energy into doing something special for someone, only to be disappointed when they didn't seem as appreciative or excited by your efforts as you had anticipated?

Do you ever feel like your partner is trying to be there for you but they're just not getting it quite right?

Do *you* ever feel like you want to help and support your partner, but you're not quite sure how?

If this sort of thing happens regularly, you and your partner might tend to speak different love languages.

WHAT ARE LOVE LANGUAGES?

Your "love language" is the way that you naturally express and experience love.

The phrase "love languages" was coined by renowned marriage counselor, Dr. Gary Chapman. He suggests that there are five main love languages—words of affirmation, quality time, gifts, acts of service, and physical touch.[3]

Chapman believes that all of these love languages are important to us to some degree, but that people "speak" and understand love best through one or two primary love languages.

But if love doesn't come in a one-size-fits-all package, what does this mean for our relationships...?

It means we need to practice speaking the love languages that are most meaningful to our partners. It also means we need to learn to "hear the love" better when our partner's care for us in the way that comes most naturally to them.

So what do these five love languages actually look like in action? Here are a few more details.

1. WORDS OF AFFIRMATION

As it turns out, actions *don't* always speak louder than words!

If words of affirmation is your primary love language, then compliments and other words of love, respect, affection, and encouragement mean a great deal to you.

Hearing "I love you" is important to you. Hearing *why* you are loved is also very important to you. Harsh words and insults can wound you deeply and you do not forget them easily.

Ways to speak this love language

If words of affirmation are important to your partner (and, let's face it, genuine and thoughtful words of affirmation are pretty much important to *everyone* at some level) look for ways to encourage them. Here are some questions that may help you figure out how to do that sincerely and meaningfully:

- What are they skilled at? Tell them.
- Have they done a particularly good job at something? Tell them and thank them.
- Have they put a lot of time and effort into something? Acknowledge that.
- How do they make the lives of other people better? Tell them.
- Praise or compliment them in front of other people.
- What have you learned from spending time with them? Tell them.
- Do you like spending time with them? Tell them.
- Do you appreciate something? Tell them and thank them.
- Do you like something about the way they look? Tell them.
- Do you love them or miss them? Do you desire them? TELL THEM.

2. QUALITY TIME

If you highly value quality time, nothing says "I love you" like other people spending time with you and giving you their complete attention.

It's very important to you that other people are there for you. It's even better if they can put other tasks on hold and really focus on you.

When others are distracted, postpone dates, or don't listen well to you, you can feel especially hurt.

Ways to speak this love language

Here are some good ways to spend quality time with someone:

- Have an uninterrupted and focused conversation

- Have a face-to-face conversation
- Give them your whole attention (stop trying to do other things while you're together and just focus on *being* with them)
- Spend one-on-one time together
- Ask them questions about things that are important to them
- Do something with them that they enjoy (play a board game, listen to a podcast, watch a TV show, go on a hike, etc.)
- Spend time together, even if it's just running errands

3. GIFTS

If gifts is one of your primary love languages you thrive on receiving presents and other physical tokens of love.

When others give you gifts or surprise you with thoughtful gestures, those things help you feel understood and cherished. To you, those gifts or gestures are tangible expressions of effort and care.

When people miss your birthday and other important anniversaries (or when they give you thoughtless or inconsiderate gifts) it can hurt you deeply.

Ways to speak this love language

If your partner or someone else you love thrives on receiving gifts, look for ways to "speak love" to them in this way. Here are some ideas for how to do that:

- Put care and thought into their gifts on special occasions
- Give them flowers, gifts, or other gestures every so often "just because"
- Write them cards and notes
- Buy them their favorite snacks, or cook them their favorite meal
- Look for small tokens or trinkets that will let your partner know you're thinking about them. (Giving gifts is not all about spending

money. For example, if you spend a Saturday hiking without your partner for some reason, pick up a flower, pebble, or other token that reminded you of your partner and give it to them.)

- Celebrate milestones with tangible "gifts" or "experiences". (For example, the first month that I made more than $100 selling books off my website, my husband bought a $100 bottle of champagne to celebrate. Now, gift giving is *not* my primary love language. I love getting them, of course, but I don't *need* them to feel loved. To be honest, when Mike pulled out the bottle I was largely horrified by his extravagance, but I still smile now when I remember it.)

4. ACTS OF SERVICE

If you speak this language, you feel most loved when others do practical things to help or serve you—when they ease the burden of your responsibilities.

Taking out the trash, doing the grocery shopping, watching the kids, making dinner, paying bills... there are many ways to show love to someone who highly values acts of service.

When others appear lazy, don't follow through on their commitments, or make more work for you, you feel disregarded and unloved.

Ways to speak this love language

Acts of service is a fairly flexible love language. To speak it well, you just need to look for ways to ease burdens, save someone time and energy, or do something meaningful for them. For example, you could:

- Help with chores and housework (do something for them that's normally their responsibility)
- Babysit (there are very few things more valuable to a busy parent of young children than a couple of free hours)
- Make or buy a meal for them

- Help them out financially by paying for groceries, travel costs, or other necessities (an especially good one if finances are tight).
- Surprise them with unexpected and thoughtful gifts. Any time you spend selecting and sending gifts, notes, or other tokens of love, appreciation, and encouragement is an act of service as well.
- In a similar vein, spending time talking to your partner can be an act of service in and of itself. If you are prioritizing communication with your partner—spending time listening to their joys and frustrations, and (when invited) trying to help them brainstorm ways to manage their problems and worries—you are serving them.

5. PHYSICAL TOUCH

If this is one of your primary love languages you are probably a "touchy" person.

You love to give and receive hugs, pats on the back, massages, and other types of thoughtful and appropriate touches. These touches speak to you of connection, concern, understanding, and caring.

When those you love don't connect with you in this way, you can feel distant from them, disconnected, and unloved.

The love language of physical touch is often confused with "sex." While sex may feel very important to someone whose primary love language is touch, this love language is much broader than that. Those who feel nourished by touch can feel cherished by a simple hand hold.

Ways to speak this love language

How to speak this love language directly is obvious. Give cuddles, hugs, kisses, pats on the back, holding hands, massages, head-rubs, gentle passing touches, sex... pretty much anything involving (desired) touch will speak love to someone who highly values physical touch.

But there are some less obvious ways to speak this love language, too. Here are some ways you can speak this language indirectly, if you're in a long distance relationship or not physically together in the moment:

- Use non-verbal body language that emphasizes care and affection
- *Tell* them that you'd love to give them a hug or a kiss
- Use the hug and kiss emoticons in messaging programs
- Email (or print out and send) special photos of the two of you together to remind your partner of warm, happy moments.
- Send a letter or gift (maybe a piece of your clothing) that is scented with your perfume or cologne.
- Give them special stuffed animal or pillow to cuddle
- Get them a certificate for a massage.

YOUR TASK THIS WEEK

What were you thinking as you read the descriptions above? Which love language would you guess is *your* primary one? What about your partner? How similar are you in what makes you feel most loved?

After reading the descriptions above, you may already be able to identify your primary love language (or your top two). Sometimes, however, a questionnaire can be helpful to confirm your instincts or suggest an option you hadn't considered.

This week, you have two tasks to complete.

Fill out the love languages questionnaire

Even if you think you already know your primary love language, try this:

1. Go to http://www.5lovelanguages.com
2. Click the appropriate buttons to take the assessment.
3. Fill out the 30-item questionnaire.

Answer these questions

Now, answer the following questions and make some notes.

1. What is your primary love language?

____

____

____

____

____

2. Do you have a strong love-language preference? (Is it clear that you have one preferred love language, or do you score almost equally across two or more love languages?)

____

____

____

____

____

3. Do you agree with the results of the love languages questionnaire?

____

____

____

____

____

4. What do you think is your partner's primary love language?

____

____

____

____

____

5. Describe times when you have felt well-loved by your partner or others.

____

____

____

____

____

6. If you and your partner have different love languages, what sorts of misunderstandings, hurt feelings, or conflict might arise from these different preferences?

____

____

____

____

____

7. List three ways you could show your partner you care for them this week by speaking a love language that's important to them.

____

____

____

____

____

DURING YOUR DATE

During your date this week, talk about love languages and what you've been learning. Here are some things to share, some questions to ask your partner, and some questions for the two of you to discuss.

Share with your partner

- Your one or two primary love languages.
- Things your partner has done that make you feel especially loved and cared for.

Ask your partner

- What are *your* one or two primary love languages?
- What is something I do (or have done) that make you feel especially cared for or encouraged?

Discuss the following

1. If you have different love languages, what sorts of misunderstandings, hurt feelings, or conflict could arise from these different preferences?
2. How and when have you found it challenging to speak each other's love language(s)?
3. What is one thing you each intend to do in the next week to speak the other person's love language?

Looking forward...

Congratulations, Week 4 is in the bag.

See you back here next week with your explorer gear on. We'll learn why making a habit of trying new things is good for us (and our relationship), and you're off on a little adventure.

WEEK 5

Go On An Adventure

This week you will learn why trying new things can make you happier and is good for your relationship. You will go on an adventure and talk about how you embrace novelty and adventure in life.

DURING MY SECOND year at university, a friend decided to have her birthday party at a local Indian restaurant.

I groaned.

Despite having spent two years of my childhood in Bangladesh (or maybe *because* of that) I was not at all keen on Indian food. I only went to her party because she was a good friend, and sometimes you have to suck it up and go the extra mile for good friends.

But, you know what? I *loved* it.

I loved it so much that the place became my new favorite restaurant. I even booked my own 21st birthday bash there a couple of years later. Indian still remains one of my favorite cuisines, today. If I hadn't branched out and tried something new, I'd still be missing out on lamb korma and naan bread.

This week we're all about trying new things and your task is to go on an adventure. Before we get into the details, however, let's look a little more at why trying new things is good for you.

WHY TRYING NEW THINGS IS GOOD FOR YOU

Yes, trying something new is a risk.

It can definitely make you more miserable in the moment. A new restaurant or dish can disappoint, singing karaoke can result in public humiliation, a movie or a play can bore us silly (Shakespeare's *A Winter's Tale*, anyone?)

But did you know that science suggests making a habit of experimenting and trying new things will make you happier in the long run?

For example, research by psychologist Rich Walker suggests that people who engage in a wider variety of life experiences are more likely to remember positive emotions and minimize negative ones than people who have fewer experiences.[4]

Here are a couple of other ways that novelty and adventuring can breed happiness.

1. Trying new things can introduce you to new pleasures and passions

Trying something new can introduce you to new pleasures to savor. I hate to think what I would have missed if I had not reluctantly gone to the Indian restaurant that night!

Taking small steps into new realms can also help you discover things that capture your imagination, fire up your passions, and help you envision new possibilities in your life.

2. Novelty causes your brain to release "reward chemicals"

When we explore and try something new, dopamine gets released in our brains.

So, what does dopamine do? It tends to make you feel more excited, energetic, curious, and positive. That's why trying something new can give you a positive boost.

3. Trying something new forces you to grow

Doing something new forces you to learn and change much more quickly than doing something you've done many times before.

New experiences and situations can broaden your worldview, change your perspective, and teach you new things. New actions can lead to new skills.

Consistently facing new challenges also helps shape your general attitude towards life—it can keep you curious, humble, and open to new ideas.

And trying new things, even if they don't go well, can boost your self-confidence and your belief in your own ability to meet challenges, rise to the occasion, and bounce back after failure.

WHY TRYING NEW THINGS IS GOOD FOR YOUR RELATIONSHIP

We've just seen why making a habit out of trying new things is good for you as an individual. As it turns out, it can be good for your relationship too, especially over time.

In the early stages of a new relationship you are flooded with dopamine and other neurotransmitters that motivate you to focus on your new partner. These chemicals all contribute to that intoxicating feeling of falling in love.

The early days of a new relationship are a time of intense and rapid change as you absorb details about your partner and get to know them. As you grow closer during this charged period, your sense of self expands as you take on your partner's perspectives, stories, and experiences.

Over time the "rush" and intoxication of new love fades, and is replaced by a quieter brand of committed attachment.

However, research suggests that couples who embrace novelty after a relationship is well established—who tend to explore new places and try new things together—tap into a dynamic similar to the one operating when they first fall in love.[5]

The excitement and learning engendered by novelty also tends to boost commitment.

Interestingly, doing different things early in a relationship (when you've been together a year or less) has almost no benefit. The relationship itself is intense and novel enough. But after the relationship is established, the relationship benefits of doing new and challenging things together are significant.

YOUR TASK THIS WEEK

Do something new together this week. Have a new adventure. If you're not sure where to start, here are some suggestions:

1. Pretend you're a tourist and go to a part of the city you've never visited before.
2. Visit a museum or an art gallery.
3. Try a new restaurant or order a new type of food.
4. Volunteer for a local shelter or charity organization, or visit a nursing home and spend time reading to residents or playing board games.
5. Learn how to do something new, and then find a way to put your new knowledge into practice.

Now, answer these questions:

1. What adventure did you choose? Did you enjoy it? Why or why not?

2. What are two other "adventures" you might like to go on in the next month?

3. We all seek out novelty in life to some extent—even routine-lovers. What types of new experiences do you tend to seek out most?
    a. Do you often branch out and drive different routes, or cook new dishes?
    b. What topics do you tend to learn new facts about easily?
    c. What types of new skills or activities do you tend to seek out?

DURING YOUR DATE

Your adventure may double as your date this week, so while you're out and about see if you can make space to discuss these questions. Otherwise, double-up on dates this week so that you can talk about how you each approach adventure. Here are some questions to get you started:

1. Did you enjoy your chosen adventure? Why, or why not?
2. Would you do it again?
3. Do you generally like doing new things or do you prefer to stick to routine?
4. Tell me about a time you tried something new and loved it/it was good for you.
5. Tell me about a time you went on an adventure and it all went wrong.
6. We all seek out novelty in life to some extent—even routine-lovers. What types of new experiences do you tend to seek out most? For example:
    a. Do you often branch out and drive different routes, or cook new dishes?
    b. What topics do you tend to learn new facts about easily?
    c. What types of new skills or activities do you tend to seek out?
7. What is something new you'd like to do together someday?
8. What is something new you'd like to do together next month?

Looking forward...

I hope you had fun this week! Next week is "book club" week, so if you haven't already checked out the recommended list in the next chapter or picked a different book, you might want to do that now.

WEEK 6

Lit Pick For Two

This week you will run an intimate Book-Club-For-Two. You will explore how and why reading is good for you and your relationship. Then you will both read the same book, story, or comic book, and talk it over.

I'M SO EXCITED about this week's topic, I can't even tell you! Settling down with a good book is one of the things that I *loooooove* doing.

To be honest, I'd read voraciously even if it *wasn't* good for me, but science is the icing on the cake in this case. Did you know that reading is good for you in all sorts of ways? Here are just a few of them.

THREE WAYS READING IS GOOD FOR YOU

Reading helps your brain function better

The phrase "use it or lose it" doesn't just apply to muscle tone—it also holds true for your brain.

Reading stimulates your brain in a way that watching television doesn't. It makes your brain work in ways that help improve brain function.[6]

For example, reading a book improves your ability to focus and concentrate over time (a skill that decays in people who often try to multi-task or skim through lots of information on a computer screen.)

Research also suggests that reading regularly and/or focusing on other forms of challenging mental stimulation (like puzzles or crosswords) can help prevent or slow memory loss and the progress of dementia or Alzheimer's in later life.

Reading can reduce stress

When you become absorbed in something that you're reading, you "switch channels" in your brain. You become transported to another world, or lost in the details of something completely different than the responsibilities, worries, and distractions that normally occupy your thoughts.

As this happens, you often relax.

Research on readers has revealed significant drops in their heart rate and muscle tension after just a few minutes of reading.[7] Reading spiritual texts, in particular, have been found to lower blood pressure and bring about a sense of calm and purpose.

Reading can boost empathy

When you read, you are doing more than just spending some time away from your own perspective and problems, you are spending that time exploring *other's* perspectives and problems.

Reading fiction and memoirs, in particular, can help you better understand other people's challenges, motivations, and beliefs. This ability to understand and adopt other's perspectives is the cornerstone of empathy, and it is a crucial skill in communicating well and building successful relationships.

Some of these benefits don't hold true for all books, of course. I doubt that reading thrillers really helps most people relax, and reading a lot of the type of romance novels that Harlequin churns out (the type featuring muscle-bound men, virgin women just waiting to be swept off their feet, and happily ever after) definitely *won't* help your real-life relationship in the long run. But the general take-away is this: Reading books is good for you.

So, this week, that's you're going to do—read the same book and have a book-club date. And, remember, even if this doesn't sound like your idea of a fun things to do, it's good to get into the habit of trying new things in life.

Book-Club-For-Two will give you something new to focus on and talk about, and it will help you learn more about how your partner sees the world. Win-win!

YOUR TASK THIS WEEK

Your task this week is simple.

- Pick a book you will both read.
- Read it.
- Then, gather up some wine, ice-cream, mood lighting and/or chocolate and discuss it.

Do you have a book you've been meaning to find time to read? Great. As long as you have something in mind and you can convince your partner to read it too, you're all set.

If you don't already have a book in mind, jump down to the recommended reading at the end of this chapter. There are 20 good books listed there.

DURING YOUR DATE

Many books have reading-club guides included at the back or discussions questions available for download online. You can print one of those out and use it to help you talk about your book.

In case there isn't a good discussion guide available, here are a few questions you can use to kick-start your book-club date:

1. How would you rate this book on Amazon (out of five stars)? Why?

2. What's something that stood out to you in this book—something that you liked or that surprised you?
3. If you could change something about this book, what would it be?
4. If you could ask the author something, what would it be?
5. What is something you may take away from reading this book? Did it teach you anything? Move you? Change any of your views or thoughts?

20 BOOKS I RECOMMEND

There should be something on this recommended reading list for pretty much everyone. There are relationship self-help books, parenting books, novels, young adult fiction, and non-fiction titles on here. There are books that generally appeal to both men and women. There's even one novel (Illuminae) that's part comic.

Book descriptions are below. First, however, a quick guide for those of you who have no idea where to start.

If you want...

1. A book that will help give you a deeper, richer, perspective on life... choose *Tiny Beautiful Things.*
2. A book to improve your communication and relationship... choose *The 5 Love Languages, The Seven Principles*, or *Hold Me Tight.*
3. Books men should especially enjoy... choose *Ender's Game, Game of Thrones, Illuminae, Station Eleven,* or *The Hunger Games.*
4. Something to help you think differently about parenting... choose *Bringing Up Bebe* or *All Joy And No Fun.*
5. Something to help you become a better parent... choose *The Whole-Brain Child.*
6. A book that will help inspire you to live more creatively, passionately, or happily... choose *Big Magic* or *Stumbling On Happiness.*

RELATIONSHIP BOOKS

The Five Love Languages (Gary Chapman)
When I asked my friends and regular readers which relationship book had impacted them most, this best-seller was the book most people mentioned.

Dr. Gary Chapman outlines 5 love languages (ways of showing and receiving love) that will help you experience deeper and richer levels of intimacy with your partner. If you want to delve more deeply into the topic of love languages than we already have in this series, this is the book for you.

The Seven Principles For Making Marriage Work (John Gottman and Nan Silver)
John Gottman is a professor of psychology and the founder and director of the Seattle Marital and Family Institute. This highly rated book—based on decades of clinical and research experience—focuses on seven principles for building harmonious and strong relationships. It includes questionnaires and exercises.

Hold Me Tight: Seven Conversations For A Lifetime Of Love (Sue Johnson)
The book is based on the Emotionally Focused Therapy model. Dr. Sue Johnson aims to help couples establish safe emotional connection and strengthen their attachment bond. The book focuses on key moments in a relationship (from "recognizing the demon dialogue" to "revisiting a rocky moment") and uses them as touch points to help couples have seven healing conversations.

PARENTING BOOKS

The Whole-Brain Child: 12 Revolutionary Strategies To Nurture Your Child's Developing Mind (Daniel Siegel and Tina Payne Bryson)
This practical book explains how a child's brain is wired and how it matures. The "upstairs brain" which balances and regulates emotions and helps guide decisions is under construction until the mid-twenties. And,

especially in young children, the right brain and emotions tend to dominate the logic of the left brain.

The book includes lots of examples and focuses on 12 strategies that foster healthy brain development and calmer, happier children.

All Joy And No Fun: The Paradox Of Modern Parenthood (Jennifer Senior)
Award-winning journalist Jennifer Senior explores how children reshape their parent's lives, marriages, jobs, habits, friendships, and identities. She argues that changes in the last half century have radically altered and complicated the current roles of parents.

This book will make you breathe a sigh of relief as you reconsider some of our culture's most basic beliefs about parenting, while illuminating the how children also deepen and add purpose to our lives.

Bringing Up Bebe: One American Mother Discovers The Wisdom Of French Parenting (Pamela Druckerman)
When American journalist Pamela Druckerman had a baby in Paris she didn't aspire to become a "French parent." But then she noticed that French children slept through the night by two or three months old. They ate brie and braised leeks. They played happily by themselves, but were still boisterous, curious, and creative. Why? How?

This is a fascinating and funny read for anyone in a cross-cultural relationship, especially for couples who have (or are intending to have) kids. You're unlikely to walk away without having at least one of your assumptions about how parenting "should" be done deeply challenged.

How Children Succeed: Grit, Curiosity, And The Hidden Power Of Character (Paul Tough)
Paul Tough argues that the characteristics that really help children succeed have less to do with intelligence than they do with skills like perseverance, curiosity, optimism, and self-control. This provocative and hopeful book uses research to peel back some of the mysteries of character, and how to help instill and shape it in our children.

ESSAYS

Tiny Beautiful Things (Cheryl Strayed)
Cheryl Strayed is better known for her bestselling memoir, *Wild*, but this is my favorite book of hers. It is a collection of *Dear Sugar* advice columns covering birth, sex, death, and everything in between. It is honest, incisive, funny, beautifully written, and very powerful. You'll find lots of things to discuss and think about in this collection!

NON-FICTION

Stumbling On Happiness (Daniel Gilbert)
At times (or, uh, most days) we all make certain choices that we regret later, whether that's to overeat, over-drink, or over-spend. And overall, we humans are remarkably bad at predicting what will actually make us happy in life. In this smart and funny book, Harvard psychologist Dr. Daniel Gilbert looks into the neuroscience behind this phenomenon.

Outliers: The Story Of Success (Malcolm Gladwell)
In this entertaining book, Gladwell argues that superstars are "the beneficiaries of hidden advantages and extraordinary opportunities and cultural legacies that allow them to learn and work hard and make sense of the world in ways others cannot." Along the way, Gladwell explores the sorts of backgrounds that spawn software billionaires, star soccer players, and great rock bands.

Big Magic: Creative Living Beyond Fear (Elizabeth Gilbert)
Elizabeth Gilbert (of *Eat, Pray, Love* fame) turns her self-deprecating humour and own authentic incisiveness to debunking the myth of the tormented artist. She deftly tackles the unrealistic expectations and unnecessary melodrama often attached the concept of making a living creatively, and offers some straight-talking advice on how to keep fear in proper perspective.

This book is light, playful, funny, and encouraging. A great read for anyone creative (which Gilbert would argue is all of us).

NOVELS

Station Eleven (Emily St. John Mandel)
Multiple, connected tales unfold in this beautifully written, suspenseful, stick-with-you novel. Days before civilization is wiped out by a flu pandemic, a famous Hollywood actor collapses and dies onstage. Years afterwards, a small Shakespeare troupe roams the land, striving for more than mere survival.

Illuminae (Amie Kaufman & Jay Kristoff)
In the morning, Kady thought breaking up with Ezra was the hardest thing she'd have to do. In the afternoon, her planet was invaded. The year is 2575 and two rival mega-corporations are at war over a planet that's little more than an ice-covered speck at the edge of the universe. This is a fast-paced and clever novel about lives interrupted, the price of truth, and the courage of everyday heroes.

A Game Of Thrones: A Song Of Ice And Fire (George. R. R. Martin)
Long ago, in a forgotten time, the seasons were thrown out of balance. In a land where summers can last decades and winters a lifetime, trouble is brewing...

The plot and the world Martin builds are too complex to effectively summarize here, but if you like fantasy and long, involved, lush novels, this is a book for you. It is the first in what has been hailed as an epic series.

Ender's Game (Orson Scott Card)
In order to develop a secure defense against a hostile alien race's next attack, government agencies breed child geniuses and train them as soldiers. A brilliant young boy, Andrew "Ender" Wiggin lives with his kind but distant parents, his sadistic brother Peter, and the person he loves more than anyone else, his sister Valentine. Peter and Valentine were candidates for the soldier-training program but didn't make the cut—young Ender is the Wiggin drafted to the orbiting Battle School for rigorous military training...

There is a reason this book won both the Nebula and the Hugo Award. Fantasy and Sci-Fi are not my favorite genres, but I found this book utterly fascinating and have read it more than once.

Code Name Verity (Elizabeth Wein)
Oct. 11th, 1943—A British spy plane crashes in Nazi-occupied France. Its pilot and passenger are best friends. Can both girls survive?...

Some novels stick with you in vivid detail long after you finish them. For me, this book has been one of those. Winner of the Michael L. Printz Award, it was reviewed as "a fiendishly-plotted mind game of a novel" by the New York Times. It is a gripping tale of danger, resolve, and survival that shows just how far true friends will go to save each other.

The Hunger Games (Suzanne Collins)
You've doubtless all seen the movies, and Amazon.com bills this as "the book no one can stop talking about" so I probably don't even need to include a teaser description, but here's one anyway: "In the ruins of a place once known as North America lies the nation of Panem, a shining Capitol surrounded by twelve outlying districts. The Capitol is harsh and cruel and keeps the districts in line by forcing them all to send one boy and one girl between the ages of twelve and eighteen to participate in the annual Hunger Games, a fight to the death on live TV..."

I will say that (unlike some other popular book-phenomenon out there—*Twilight* and *50 Shades Of Grey,* I'm looking at you) The Hunger Games is well-written and worth all the hype and attention it has received.

The Time Traveler's Wife (Audrey Niffenegger)
I first read The Time Traveler's Wife in Heathrow airport while I was en-route from Kenya to Los Angeles. The story kept me completely engrossed and entertained for most of a six-hour layover (which given the din and clamour of that airport, is no small feat).

The story rotates around the relationship between Clare and Henry. They've known each other since Clare was six and Henry was thirty-six, and were married when Clare was twenty-three and Henry thirty-one. Impossible, right? Except that Henry (who is one of the first people diagnosed with Chrono-Displacement Disorder) periodically finds himself misplaced in time, pulled to moments of emotional gravity in his life, past and future. His disappearances are spontaneous, his experiences unpredictable, alternately harrowing and amusing. The book is totally original and emotionally rich.

The Help (Kathryn Stockett)
Jackson, Mississippi. 1962. Several black maids and a young white college graduate form an unlikely and dangerous alliance to write a tell-all book about working as a black maid in the South. The collaboration forever alters their lives and the small town in which they all live.

This book is a seamless intertwining of personal and political history during the nascent days of the civil rights movement in America. It is also, still, a challenging and uncomfortable read.

The Husband's Secret (Liane Moriarty)
Imagine that your husband wrote you a letter to be opened after his death. Imagine, too, that the letter contains his deepest, darkest secret—something with the potential to destroy not just the life you built together, but the lives of others as well. Imagine, then, that you stumble across that letter while your husband is still very much alive...

Set in middle class Australia, this deceptively-rich page-turner explores the power of secrets and how well it is ever possible to really know our spouses, and ourselves.

LOOKING FORWARD...

I hope you had a good time this week reading and connecting. See you back here next week when we look at whether opposites really attract, and what the best formula is for a happy couple. Along the way, you'll identify your own personality type.

WEEK 7

Let's Get Personal(ity)

This week you will look at whether opposites really attract, and what the best formula is for a happy couple. You will use a questionnaire to identify your personality type and discuss your profile.

MY PARENTS HAD been married for nearly 20 years before they figured out that they had very different personalities.

They believed a lot of the same things and held many of the same values, so they had always assumed that they were similar in every other way as well.

The year I turned 16, we were living in Zimbabwe. That summer, the five of us went on a family road trip in a station wagon. And what entertainment did my parents packed along for us to listen to in the car while we drove around Africa looking for stone ruins in the middle of nowhere??

A series of tapes on personality differences.

(Here I will pause for a moment so that you can reconsider whether you really had it so bad as a teenager after all.)

What I remember most clearly about this trip is not the ruins of Great Zimbabwe. No. I remember lying sprawled in the back of that station wagon with my brother and sister while my parents laughed and laughed as they learned that they were really very different in how they generally approached life.

My detailed-oriented, logical, conscientious father and my sunny, social, never-let-the-facts-stand-in-the-way-of-a-good-story mother.

Who would have guessed?

The thing is, *they* didn't guess. Not for years. Because they were so similar in so many other ways (beliefs, values, approaches to money, family, and commitment) figuring out that they were actually very different in how they naturally approached situations, made decisions, and related to people was a revelation to them. And learning about these differences helped them understand each other better and communicate more effectively.

Total relationship win.

So, I've got some good news for you...

You can learn more about personalities before you've been married for twenty years and *without* trekking across Zimbabwe with your entire family in tow.

In fact, that's just what we're going to do this week.

WHAT IS PERSONALITY?

Before we get to the really fun stuff, let's define personality so that we're all on the same page.

We all have certain consistent tendencies in how we think, feel, act and react. These patterns form the basic framework of our "personality," and they tend to stay fairly stable and consistent over time.

A "personality trait" refers to an enduring personal characteristic that influences behavior in a variety of situations. For example, some people tend to be quiet and reserved in new situations or big groups. Others tend to talk more and connect socially quickly and easily.

DO OPPOSITES REALLY ATTRACT?

Have you ever heard the saying "opposites attract?"

What about the saying "like attracts like?"

And here's the million-dollar question: When it comes to relationships, will we generally be happier with someone who is similar to us or different from us?

There is no simple answer to this question, but here are a few things to think about.

We tend to be attracted to people who have similar attitudes, values, and beliefs to ours

We are often drawn to people who share similar values, beliefs, and experiences to ours.

We understand them more easily. We agree with them. We instinctively tend to like them more. This is the "like attracts like" dynamic.

We generally learn something about someone's basic attitudes, beliefs, and life experiences fairly early on in a relationship. However, as was the case for my parents, personality-related characteristics can take longer to unfold and understand. They may not play a substantial role until later on in a relationship.

We can be attracted to people who have different personalities than us

We can be drawn to people who display very different demeanors or approaches to life than our own. For example, a bubbly extravert can find a thoughtful introvert mysterious and intriguing. The introvert can find the charming socialite fun and compelling. This is the dynamic that spawned the saying "opposites attract."

In the early years of their relationship, couples with similar personalities may face fewer conflicts

Early on in a relationship you are getting to know each other, building intimacy, setting patterns, and sharing dreams.

During this period, connecting as a couple can be easier if your personalities are more similar.

For example, if you are both hard-wired to seek out adventure or, conversely, you both prefer the ease and routine of the tried and true, you'll have fewer situations where you want different things. If you both prefer crashing out on the couch and watching movies rather than going out dancing with a group of friends, there is less to argue over.

However, couples in mid-life may struggle more if they're very similar in personality

As relationships progress, different challenges enter the picture.

Couples have children, change jobs, make big financial decisions, face major disappointments and challenges, need to care for aging parents, etc.

Couples who share very similar personalities may have a more difficult time multi-tasking to meet all these demands, whereas partners with different personalities have an easier time "balancing each other out."

For example, if neither partner is detail oriented, then managing finances and paying bills might become a bone of contention. If both parents are highly introverted, parenting children will exhaust both parties and can lead to more arguments and resentments.

WHAT IS THE BEST PERSONALITY FORMULA FOR A HAPPY COUPLE?

You've probably guessed what I'm going to say by now: There is no one formula that guarantees a happy, healthy couple at all stages of your relationship.

If you and your partner are similar in personality you may have fewer tension points overall, but find yourself arguing *because* you're so similar in some ways.

If you are different in personality, you may puzzle and annoy each other more. However, those very differences may enable you to problem-solve life together more effectively.

Perhaps the best thing you can do when it comes to personality is learn more

If you understand yourself and you know your partner well, too, you will be able to support and appreciate each other better. You will be able to navigate your differences or collective weaknesses more effectively, and head off some of your disagreements before they become major conflicts.

Who wouldn't want that?

So, this week we'll be using a personality framework called the Enneagram to help you learn more about your personality and your partner's.

WHAT IS THE ENNEAGRAM?

The Enneagram is a nine-sided figure that outlines a spectrum of possible personality types. The picture on the next page helps explain the different personality types.

Take a couple of minutes to look this over. Read about the nine different types.

Which type (or two types) would you guess you are? Which type(s) would you guess your partner is?

OK, when you've had a good look at the Enneagram types, it's time to do this week's task.

THE PEACEMAKER
THE MEDIATOR
9
THE CHALLENGER
THE PROTECTOR
8
1
THE REFORMER
THE PERFECTIONIST
THE ENTHUSIAST
THE EPICURE
7
2
THE HELPER
THE GIVER
THE LOYALIST
THE SKEPTIC
6
3
THE ACHIEVER
THE PERFORMER
5
THE INVESTIGATOR
THE OBSERVER
4
THE INDIVIDUALIST
THE ROMANTIC

The 9 Enneagram Personality Types

Here is a brief description of each of the Enneagram types.

1. ***The Reformer/Perfectionist:*** Often principled, serious, and self-controlled. Can be critical. Pays attention to right and wrong, and being good. Spends energy on trying to improve.

2. ***The Helper/Giver:*** Often connected, empathetic, loving, and generous. Can be possessive and intrusive. Pays attention to the wants and needs of others and being appreciated. Spends energy on giving and helping.

3. ***The Achiever/Performer:*** Often adaptable, pragmatic, charming, and charismatic. Can be image-conscious and arrogant. Pays attention to what brings success and approval. Spends energy on standing out, and achieving goals, tasks, and prestige.

4. ***The Individualist/Romantic:*** Often introspective, creative, and unique. Can be temperamental and self-indulgent. Pays attention to

their own identity and experience, and what is missing. Spends energy on seeking out the most unique, special and fulfilling.

5. ***The Investigator/Observer:*** Often analytical, innovative, and speculative. Can be secretive and detached. Pays attention to the expectations of others. Spends energy on becoming self-sufficient, private, and acquiring knowledge.
6. ***The Loyalist/Skeptic:*** Often responsible, committed, vigilant, and compliant. Can be nervous and suspicious. Pays attention to hazards and threats and group dynamics. Spends energy on being vigilant, questioning.
7. ***The Enthusiast/Epicure:*** Often spontaneous, fun-loving, and versatile. Can be hyperactive, scattered, and excessive. Pays attention to seeking stimulation and experience, and to limits and constraints. Spends energy on seeking out interesting ideas and pleasurable experiences.
8. ***The Challenger/Protector:*** Often self-confident, dominant, and assertive. Can be pushy and forceful. Pays attention to those who needs attention, and to power and control. Spends energy on being powerful, leadership, and protecting and fighting.
9. ***The Peacemaker/Mediator:*** Often pleasant, peaceful, reassuring, and accepting. Can be passive and negligent. Pays attention to conflict and discomfort. Spends energy on other people and avoiding or preventing conflicts.

YOUR TASK THIS WEEK

Your task this week has two parts. First, you'll use an online questionnaire to identify your Enneagram Type. Then you'll take some time to figure out (a) if you agree with these results, and (b) what this means in your relationship.

Find your Enneagram Type

1. Go to the Eclectic Energies Enneagram Test page: https://www.eclecticenergies.com/enneagram/test.php
2. Choose to take the Classical Enneagram Test
3. Answer each question. This will take about 10-15 minutes, more if you pause to think deeply about some questions.
4. After you're finished you'll be presented with your results. Click to read up on your main type.
    a. You can find more information about the types on the Eclectic Energies site here: https://www.eclecticenergies.com/enneagram/. However, I find the Eclectic Energies descriptions of the types somewhat harsh and confronting. You will find more balanced (less negative) descriptions of the types on the Enneagram Institute site here: https://www.enneagraminstitute.com/type-descriptions/.
5. Now, google your "wing type" (the test won't link straight to a description of your wing type the same way that it does for your main type) and read some alternative descriptions of wing types as well.

Answer these questions

Now, spend some time answering the following questions and making notes.

1. What is your main type? (Summarize what this means in a way that makes sense to you. How would you explain the characteristics of this type to someone else?)

____

____

____

____

____

2. What is your wing type? What does that mean?

3. What was your 2nd highest scoring type?

4. How does this type "fit" you? Describe some things you commonly do and feel that that are in line with your type.

5. What are some ways that this type doesn't "fit" you? Describe some things you commonly do and feel that that are *not* in line with your type.

DURING YOUR DATE

During your date this week, share about your types and discuss your answers to the questions above. After that, think about the common strengths and weaknesses of your type and your partner's type and answer these questions together:

1. How could your two types complement each other and benefit you as a couple?
2. What are negative patterns that might develop, or common conflicts that people of these two types may experience in their relationship?

Looking forward...

There was a lot of information to take in this week, so well done for focusing and taking it all in.

See you back here next week. We'll be looking together at one of my favorite (and powerful) positive psychology topics—it's a surefire way to make us happier!

WEEK 8

Be Grateful For The Good Things

This week you will look at how gratitude makes us happier. You will practice a gratitude exercise and discuss how you experience gratitude in your life.

MOST DAYS WE experience both good and bad events—pleasures and frustrations, blessings and trials, boosts and setbacks.

But when our friends and family ask how our day is going (or how it's been), how often do we talk about the frustrations before the joys?

On a day-to-day basis, we seem to be better at focusing on and remembering negative experiences rather than positive ones. We can view the more distant past (the good-old-days) through rose-colored glasses. However, most of us are more primed to remember the bad things about the recent past, while forgetting or discounting the good things.[8]

In other words, we think a bit too much about what's going wrong in our lives and not enough about what's going right.

Of course, we *should* spend some of our time thinking and talking about the bad stuff. It makes sense to analyze things that make us frustrated, sad, or angry so that we can learn from these events and (hopefully) avoid them in the future. However, many of us spend more time focusing on the negative than what is helpful for our mood, relationships, and general outlook on life.

OK, now are you ready for some good news?

We can totally learn to fight this negativity bias and rewire our brains to think more positively! The benefits of doing this are HUGE. And it's pretty easy and fun to get started. In fact, that's exactly what we're going to do this week.

HOW GRATITUDE MAKES US HAPPIER

One of the best and easiest ways to train ourselves to pay more attention to the good stuff in life is to practice gratitude—to teach ourselves to scan our environments for good things, and to name and count our blessings.

There's a ton of research out there now demonstrating that intentionally practicing gratitude will improve our mood in the short term and make us happier over time.[9]

I'm not going to summarize all of these research studies. However, if you're anything like me, you want to know *why* and *how* things work, not just that they do.

So here a quick look at some of the different ways gratitude helps make us happier:

1. Gratitude acts like a magnifying glass, highlighting positive emotions. It also helps minimize and block negative emotions like envy, resentment, regret, and sadness.

2. Feeling grateful for something—paying attention to something that's gone well or is good—focuses you on its *value*. It reorients you to focus on what you have rather than what you don't have.

3. Feeling grateful makes you more *mindful*—it slows you down, grounds you in the moment, and helps you celebrate the present.

4. When you express appreciation, wonder, awe, or thankfulness around others it inspires and encourages them. And when you

express gratitude *to* others, you also strengthen your relationship with them.

Over time, fostering a "gratitude habit" of noticing and appreciating good things in life will:

- Make you more resistant to stress and frustrations.
- Train you to look at life through a wide-angle lens and put things in a broader perspective.
- Infuse your relationships with more positivity, satisfaction, and affection.

Those are some seriously valuable benefits for a habit that is relatively easy and enjoyable to acquire!

So, this week, we're going to practice gratitude.

HOW TO PRACTICE GRATITUDE

Researcher and writer Robert Emmons calls gratitude a "felt sense of wonder, thankfulness, and appreciation for life."[10]

This definition is pretty broad. In practice, this means that we can pursue and express gratitude in a variety of ways. In fact, positive psychology has come up with several different exercises to encourage us to do just that. Two of the classic "gratitude exercises" are:

- Every evening for a week, write down three things that have gone well that day, and why.
- Every day for a week, take a moment to say thank you or recognize someone for their efforts and contributions.

Research has shown that even just a week of doing one of these two exercises will usually deliver a happiness boost that lasts for months. That's right. Months.[11]

There are plenty of other gratitude exercises out there, but here's what I would like you to try this week...

YOUR TASK THIS WEEK

1. Every day this week, write down three good things you feel grateful for. You can fill out the "Three Good Things A Day" page in this book or make your own and stick it somewhere you'll be reminded to fill it out every day (e.g., stick it to your fridge, bathroom mirror, or the back of your bedroom door.)

Feeling a bit intimidated or stuck at the thought of writing these sorts of things down? Don't feel any pressure. These things can be big or small or anything in between. Anything that is "good" in your life, or has gone well that day, or that you feel grateful for.

(This morning, after waking up to the kids five(!!!) times last night I wrote down "coffee" on my list. I wasn't being flippant—I was *really* grateful for that cup of coffee my husband made for me at 6:00am.)

So if you're feeling a bit stuck, think about things like:

- Simple pleasures (the beautiful sunset, a great cup of coffee, something beautiful you saw, smelled, touched or heard).
- Positive moments or experiences (the coworker who always smiles at you, a friend who made you laugh, a great book you're reading).
- Broader aspects of your life (your good health, a particular talent you have, the positive qualities of your partner or friend).
- Things that have gone well that day, or that you accomplished.
- Anything you're grateful for related to nature, people, work, school, life's pleasures, etc.

THREE GOOD THINGS A DAY

DURING YOUR DATE

During your date this week, talk about what it was like to do this exercise.

If you haven't already been sharing your "three good things," share some of the things you wrote down with each other now.

And here are some extra questions to discuss this week:

1. What are things you find it easy to be grateful for? What sort of "good things" do you naturally notice and appreciate in life?
2. What sort of "good things" in your life do you tend to overlook and take for granted?
3. Think of someone who has impacted or changed your life in ways that you are grateful for. Who are they? How did they influence your life?
4. What are two things you're grateful for about each other? (Remember, no pressure. These can be big or small or anything in between.)

Looking forward...

Next week is a fun one (especially for those of you who value gift giving as a love language!). We'll focus on care packages (and the fascinating story behind that term). We'll also talk about holidays and gift-giving when you were growing up and how that's influenced your hopes and expectations in this area now.

WEEK 9

Make A Care Package

This week you will learn about the origins of CARE packages and make a care package for your partner. You will talk about gift giving in your family, and how that has shaped your hopes and expectations around gifts and holidays now.

HAVE YOU EVER wondered where the phrase "care package" came from?

The original "CARE package" was created during World War II, when 22 American organizations banded together to create the charity CARE and rush life-saving "CARE packages" to survivors of WWII who were starving. These care packages were filled with things like egg and milk powder, jam, sugar, spam, margarine, and tinned steak and kidneys.

If you've ever gotten a care package before, it probably had chocolate in it rather than tinned liver. It may not have saved your life, but I'd wager it *did* bring you some happiness.

Receiving a care package from someone that you love is like getting a virtual hug with bonus chocolate.

This week we're all about those thoughtful virtual hugs. Your task is to put together a care package for your partner.

YOUR TASK THIS WEEK

This week, agree together on a monetary limit for the items in your package.

You may also want to agree on a theme beforehand (some ideas about different themes below) or agree to surprise each other.

Then get shopping or scavenging and put your package together.

Remember that the point of this task is not to buy the flashiest gift you can find, or pack your box full of a dozen trinkets. The main point is to try to find something fun, enjoyable, or thoughtful.

5 THEMES FOR CARE PACKAGES

If you're stuck for ideas, we've listed a couple of fun care package themes that you could adapt below.

Date night care package

This is a fun care package to plan with the added bonus of creating an experience you can enjoy together.

The classic version involves picking out a movie or a TV show you watch together and include the DVD (or the NetFlix code and instructions). Alternatively, you could get a new board game to try. Here are five great board games for couples:

1. Settlers Of Catan (my personal favorite)
2. Jaipur
3. Carcassone
4. Ticket To Ride
5. Hive

Then add in fun extras—wine, candles, chocolate, popcorn, etc.

[A personal word about popcorn, though. Don't buy commercial microwave popcorn. I'm no health freak. In fact, I ate two oatmeal cookies and a piece of dark chocolate for breakfast while writing this chapter. However, I do know that the chemicals in that pre-packaged and flavored microwave popcorn are a health nightmare. Search "how to make microwave popcorn in a brown paper bag" and include the home-made version.]

Breakfast on-the-go care package

If your partner isn't a morning person (or always finds themselves rushing out in the morning without having eaten breakfast), make them a care package to help start the day right.

If they work, they could take this to their office and stash their supplies there for those mornings they show up to work hungry.

Here are some things you could include:

- Granola or cereal bars
- Cashews, almonds, or other types of nuts
- Dried fruit
- Trail mix
- Small boxes of cereal
- Tea bags
- Gourmet coffee sachets
- Hot chocolate mix
- Peppermint tic tacs

Travel-essentials care package

This is a good one for someone who travels regularly.

If you travel often it gets annoying to have to pack and unpack a toiletries kit all the time. You could save your partner some time and frustration by making them a travel essentials kit that they can keep packed and ready to go.

Here are some ideas for things to include:

- Toothbrush and toothpaste
- Floss
- Lip balm
- Deodorant
- Soap

- A razor and a travel-sized can of shaving cream
- Tissues
- Empty travel-sized bottles for shampoo and conditioner
- A first-aid kit containing band-aids, antiseptic cream, ibuprofen, paracetamol, antihistamines, and cold and flu medication
- A travel sewing kit (needles, thread, safety pins, etc.)
- A stain-remover wipes or a stain remover "pen"

Things you love care package

What about filling a care package with some things you know your partner loves?

What books or magazines do they like to read? What do they watch for fun? What tea or coffee do they enjoy? What's their favorite sweet indulgence? Where is their favorite place to go to dinner (get a gift certificate)? What is something they use every day—like lip balm, makeup, or perfume?

Scavenger care package

If you're on a tight budget, consider scavenging around and putting together a care-package from things you *already* own.

You could include a book or CD your partner might like, or some cold and flu medication and a packet of instant chicken noodle soup from your pantry for the next time they come down with a cold. You could put in a stuffed animal, that bar of chocolate you've been saving for a rainy day, or make them a photo collage fancy card, or plan out a sexy follow-the-clues for them to do with you.

This gift is limited only by your imagination, your belongings, and the size of your box.

A note of caution, though! Make-your-own scavenger care packages full of pre-loved or handmade items work best if the other person knows what you are doing, so don't forget to tell your partner what the game is. Better yet, why don't you agree to *both* do make-your-own care packages?

And if you're not on a budget but a scavenger care package still sounds like fun, consider donating the money you would have spent buying items for your package straight to CARE.

Nowadays their CARE packages aren't filled with tins of liver. $29 will buy seeds for half an acre of farmland. $30 will help them construct a tippy-tap for hand-washing at a school, which helps reduce all sorts of illnesses among the children. $50 buys a lamb (yes, a real live lamb).

Pretty cool, huh? Find out more at www.care.org.

DURING YOUR DATE

During your date this week, talk about gifts and celebrations.

Some people *love* to give gifts—they spend ages thinking of the perfect present and delight in preparing them. For others, physical gifts are often an afterthought—they can find themselves scrambling around to find a gift at the last minute.

This whole topic of birthdays, holidays, parties, and gift giving can be a bit of a minefield. Especially if one half of the couple places a lot of importance on giving and receiving gifts and the other half of the couple doesn't, gifts (or the lack of them) can be the source of a great deal of disappointment, frustration, and pressure.

What can help in this area?

Well, you should know your own inclinations and habits in this area. And you should learn more about your partner's expectations and hopes.

The best way to do that is to *talk* together. Talk about how your family did presents, gifts, and parties when you were growing up. How important were they?

Talk about favorite presents you have received and given.

Talk about how you like to celebrate birthdays and significant holidays now. What sorts of gifts, rituals, or traditions are important to you?

This week, talk about all of this, and more. Here are some questions to get you started.

1. What was one of the best gifts you received when you were a child?

2. What is one of the best gifts you've received as an adult?
3. What sort of gifts did your parents and family tend to give you on your birthday, or on special holidays like Christmas, when you were growing up?
4. How did your family celebrate birthdays while you were growing up? Did you have any birthday traditions or rituals? How does your family celebrate birthdays now?
5. Tell me about one of the best birthdays you've ever had.
6. What other holidays or occasions were celebrated in your family growing up? How?
7. What are some of the best gifts you've given to others?

Looking forward…

You're two thirds of the way through this series now. Well done! Catch you back here next week for treat week and a task you're going to *love* doing.

WEEK 10

Treat Yourself

This week you will learn about the benefits of savoring, and how positive emotions do more than just make you feel good. You will treat yourself to something(s) you enjoy by designing a beautiful day out.

LAST WEEK YOU treated your partner to a care package. This week I want you to treat *yourself* to something(s) that you will enjoy—that will make you feel pleasure, happiness, joy, contentment, satisfaction, or awe.

This task is not a hard sell, right? We all like to do things that make us happy. But before you run off to book that full-body massage and a table at your favorite Thai restaurant, I want to tell you a little bit more about why doing things that make you feel happy is good for you and your relationships.

POSITIVE EMOTIONS DO MORE THAN MAKE YOU FEEL GOOD...

About fifteen years ago, a researcher named Barb Frederickson noticed a pattern in a bunch of decades-old psychology studies. That pattern was this: Putting people in a positive mood led to better outcomes.

Check this out, for example. If people unexpectedly found some money that had been hidden by researchers in a phone booth (yes, a phone booth, totally old-school) they were more likely to help a stranger in need of assistance.

The "stranger" was actually an actor, working with the researchers, of course.

And here is another one that's sort of scary: Giving a small gift of chocolates to doctors helped them make a better diagnosis![12]

Frederickson realized that positive emotions might be more than just enjoyable experiences. They might actually be *useful*. And she went on to develop one of my favorite theories—the *Broaden-and-Build* theory of positive emotion. [13]

THE BROADEN-AND-BUILD THEORY OF POSITIVE EMOTION

The Broaden-and-Build theory suggests that negative emotions (like fear, shock, sadness, and fatigue) *narrow* our attention and limit our thoughts and behaviors. This "narrowing" serves a purpose. It helps prompt us to run away from a threat, or rest, or do other things we need to do to survive or recover during times of danger or stress.

In contrast, positive emotions help us *expand* and develop (broaden and build) our social, physical, and emotional resources.

Did you know that when you're in a good mood you become more curious, playful, sociable, and creative? You become a better problem solver, too. You will persevere longer at difficult or complicated tasks. You're even a bit physically healthier, because your immune system and cardiovascular system get a boost!

This theory has plenty of research support. I won't go through all the research studies here, but the first takeaway message is this: There are a huge number of tangible benefits to happiness. What's more, these benefits are often the direct result of feeling happy, not the other way around!

But wait, there's more... This all sets you up to experience even *more* positive emotions in the future.

How?

Well, when you're being more curious, sociable, and creative, you are building supportive relationships and learning more about others and how the world works. These coping resources are building your confidence and capacity to manage future challenges, threats, and stress better.

It all creates a bit of a positive upward spiral.

YOUR TASK THIS WEEK

Your task this week is to tap into that positive upwards spiral by planning, and then doing, something that you genuinely enjoy. Follow this two-step process.

1. Design a beautiful day

Think about the week ahead of you and pick a chunk of time that you can devote to doing things you enjoy. This can be a whole day, a morning, or an evening—whatever works for your schedule.

Now, sit down and brainstorm a list of these things you love doing, that make you happy, that bring you pleasure, that help you relax, or that make you feel satisfied. Answering the following questions might help:

1. What do you love doing?

____

____

____

____

____

2. What do you enjoy that you haven't had a chance to do recently?

3. What is something you've always wanted to do but never tried?

4. What are things you know make you feel happy?

Now, plan out your beautiful day/morning/evening to include some of the things on your list. Try to include at least one thing you don't do regularly—something that feels like a special treat.

You can design this time to include your partner if you want to, but I recommend you think first about what *you* really want to do and plan for that. The whole point of this activity is for you to focus fully on something you will really enjoy.

2. Savor it

When you are actually *doing* these things, *savor* the experiences.

When you savor an experience, you engage fully in that moment. You focus, pay attention to the pleasure you are experiencing, and appreciate all the little details.

Savoring basically acts as an amplifier for positive emotions—when we mindfully focus on appreciating a moment that intensifies and lengthens our experience of the positive emotions it sparks. So, limit the selfies and concentrate on the experience.

DURING YOUR DATE

During your date this week, talk about your beautiful day, what you did, how you felt while you were living it, and how you feel about it now.

Here are some questions to get you started:

1. What did you plan for your beautiful day/morning/evening?
2. Why did you choose each element?
3. Tell me about a moment during your beautiful day that you especially enjoyed, or savored deeply.
4. Did anything surprise you about this experience?
5. What are two things you do at least once a week that bring you pleasure—that make you happy, content, or relaxed.

Looking forward...

I hope you had fun this week! See you back here next week to look at the truly surprising benefits of being kind and generous and how giving to others helps you and your important relationships.

WEEK 11

Give To Others

This week you will learn four ways that giving is good for you and 22 good ways to give to others. You will perform some random acts of kindness and discuss generosity.

LAST WEEK YOU did something nice for yourself. This week, I want you to do something nice for someone else.

In case you just heaved a sigh, or you're wondering what's in it for you, here's the cool twist on this week's assignment: *Doing kind, generous things for others is good for you.*

This is not just a religious platitude ("do unto others") packaged with the vague promise of personal reward ("it's good for you"). Nope. A growing number of research studies show that generosity also has benefits for the giver.[14] Check out these science-backed reasons to be generous and do good.

4 WAYS GIVING IS GOOD FOR YOU

Giving makes you feel happier

It appears that our brains are naturally hard-wired to reward generosity and selflessness.

A study by Jorge Moll and colleagues at the U.S. National Institutes of Health in 2006 found that when we do good things for others (such as give money to charity) it activates the region of our brain associated with pleasure, social connection, and trust.[15]

This biological reaction is reflected in our emotions. Here are two more research examples demonstrating being generous makes us feel good.

- A study by Harvard Business School professor Michael Norton and colleagues in 2008 found that giving money to someone else made participants happier than spending it on themselves (despite participants' predictions to the contrary).[16]
- Sonja Lyubomirsky (a professor of psychology at the University of California) saw similar results when she asked people to perform five acts of kindness every week for six weeks.[17]

Giving makes you physically healthier

A bunch of different research studies have linked different forms of giving to better health.

For example, studies in the medical literature have found that various forms of giving lowers the levels of the stress-related hormone cortisol, lowers blood pressure, and strengthens the immune system of the giver.

A 1999 study by Doug Oman and colleagues at the University of California found that older people who volunteered for two or more organizations were 44 percent less likely to die over a five-year period than were non-volunteers. This remained true even after controlling for variables such as age, exercise habits, general health, and negative health habits like smoking.[18]

Stephanie Brown and colleagues saw similar results in a 2003 study at the University of Michigan. They found that older individuals who provided practical help to others, or gave emotional support to their spouses, had a lower risk of dying over a five-year period than those who didn't. *Receiving* help, however, did not reduce your risk of dying.[19]

When it comes to physical health, maybe it really *is* better to give than to receive?

Giving improves your relationships

Giving to others—doing something generous or kind—promotes a sense of trust and co-operation that strengthens relationships.

A 2011 report from the National Marriage Project found that generous service was one of the key factors for a happy marriage. Elizabeth Marquardt, the associate editor of the report puts it this way: "People are happier in their marriages when they make a regular effort to serve their spouse in small ways—from making them a cup of coffee, to giving them a back rub after a long day, to going out of their way to be affectionate or forgiving."[20]

In general, "being kind and generous leads you to perceive others more positively and more charitably," writes Lyubomirsky in her book *The How of Happiness*. This "fosters a heightened sense of interdependence and cooperation in your social community."[21]

In other words, giving to others doesn't just make them feel closer and more affectionate towards us; *we* also feel closer and more affectionate towards them.

Giving makes you feel more grateful

It makes intuitive sense that *receiving* kindness or generosity can make us feel grateful. But did you know that *giving gifts* and *being generous* can make us feel more grateful, too? And (as we learned in week eight) feeling grateful also makes us happier and healthier and helps strengthen our relationships.

22 GOOD WAYS TO GIVE TO OTHERS

Do you see how giving to others—being generous and kind—feeds into a strong positive loop?

Research suggests that giving to others directly and indirectly contributes to feeling happier, being healthier, living longer, and having stronger and more positive relationships.

Remember Martin Seligman (the guy who developed the strengths framework we looked at in weeks 1 and 2)? Well, he's done a bunch of research in other areas related to wellbeing and happiness too, and he has this to say about kindness:

> *"We scientists have found that doing a kindness produces the single most reliable momentary increase in well-being of any exercise we have tested... Here is the exercise: find one wholly unexpected kind thing to do tomorrow and just do it. Notice what happens to your mood."*[22]

So, if you're feeling all inspired to be kind and generous now but don't quite know where to start, here are some ideas for how you can give to others:

1. Buy someone a gift.
2. Give money to a charity. Select some organization, project, or individual to support in some way.
3. Give money to a friend who is struggling to make ends meet or crowd-sourcing a project or an adoption.
4. Leave an unusually large tip, or pay someone else's bill at a restaurant.
5. Donate your time (e.g., work at a soup kitchen, help a child with their homework, visit an elderly relative, help a neighbor with some chores, etc.).
6. Take a cake, cookies, or a meal to a friend or acquaintance.

7. Serve someone in a small way (e.g., get them a cup of coffee, do a household chore that's normally their responsibility, run an errand for them, etc.).
8. Befriend a lonely person or hang out with the person who just moved to town.
9. Write a colleague or acquaintance a recommendation on LinkedIn or another professional networking site.
10. Babysit for friends with children.
11. Celebrate someone else's success or good news.
12. Compliment a stranger.
13. Listen to someone who needs to talk.
14. Participate in an event that someone else is organizing (organizers are often nervous that no one will show up or their event will be a bust).
15. Call your parents/someone and tell them you love them.
16. Leave a thoughtful comment on someone's blog or social media post.
17. Leave a positive review online for a book, restaurant, or experience you enjoyed.
18. Tell someone they look lovely today.
19. Give away some of your possessions (when was the last time you cleaned out your closet, anyway?)
20. Email good photos of other people to the person in the image (or make paper copies of them and send them).
21. Encourage others—tell people what they're good at, how they shine, or other things you really appreciate about them.
22. Send a thank you letter to someone (e.g., think of someone who has influenced your life for good and write them a letter or email to tell them what they did for you and thank them).

YOUR TASK THIS WEEK

This week, do at least three kind or generous things for other people.

At least two of them should be for people *other* than your partner.

DURING YOUR DATE

During your date, tell each other how you were generous or kind this week and whether you noticed yourself feeling any different afterwards.

Then discuss some of the following questions:

1. What is one way you find it easy to be kind to others?
2. What's one way you find it difficult or exhausting to be kind to others?
3. Do you find it easiest to be generous with your time, energy, or money? What about hardest?
4. Do you have routines or other structures in your life that help prompt you to be generous with your time, energy or money? (E.g., do you volunteer twice a month? Do you donate to charity by direct deposit?)
5. Tell me about a memorable time someone was generous or kind to *you.*

Looking forward...

Next week is our last week together, and you will get to "choose your own adventure." See you back here then.

WEEK 12

Choose Your Own Adventure

This week you will review everything you've covered in this series. You will choose one topic to dig deeper in, and you will talk about your "take-aways" for the future.

CONGRATULATIONS ON ARRIVING at week 12 in this series! Well done. That's three months of sustained commitment to deepening and strengthening your relationship.

You've been on quite a journey during the last 11 weeks.

You've delved into strengths and personality, humor and communication, literature and adventures.

You've also explored gratitude, giving, and experiencing positive emotions—all of which have been shown to improve wellbeing and happiness.

This week, we're not going to focus on something brand new. Instead I want you to pause, catch your breath, and review what you've already covered.

WHY REVIEW?

Review and reflection is essential for real learning. And "real learning"—the type of learning that improves your relationship and life—is what I really hope you'll be taking away from these 12 weeks.

During the past 11 weeks, I hope that you have had fun and learned some new things about your partner and yourself.

Moving forward, I also hope that some of the frameworks and tools (strengths, personality, love languages) we have explored will help you continue to deepen and strengthen your relationship.

And I hope that you experience more gratitude and savor more positive emotions in the coming months.

So, let's pause for a moment to review what we've covered during this series.

SUMMARY: THE DEEPER DATES FOR COUPLES SERIES

Here is a list of all we have covered in this series. As you look this over, think about which topics you enjoyed the most. Also think about which particular topic you might want to revisit. Your task this week will be to "choose your own adventure"—to pick one of these topics to dig into and review in detail.

[Week 1] Name Your Strengths: What are your strengths? You have more strengths than you might think—probably more than you know. This week you began the process of identifying your personal strengths and labeling them.

[Week 2] Explore Your Strengths: How do your strengths work together in your relationship? We used a questionnaire to explore your strengths profile. You shared your signature strengths with each other and explored how those strengths can complement each other.

[Week 3] Share Something Funny: How important is it for couples to find the same things funny? This week we explored sense of humor "compatibility" and when having a different sense of humor can cause big problems in a relationship. You shared things you find funny.

[Week 4] Learn To Speak The Language Of Love: What is your love language? We used a questionnaire to identify your primary love language(s), and looked at your similarities and differences, and ways to speak different love languages well.

[Week 5] Go On An Adventure: Why is trying new things good for us? You learned why trying new things can make us happier and is good for our relationships. You went on an adventure and talked about how you embrace novelty and adventure in your lives.

[Week 6] Lit Pick For Two: We explored how you like to spend your free time, and how and why reading is good for you and your relationship. You both read the same book, story, or comic book, and talked about it.

[Week 7] Let's Get Personal(ity): What is your personality? What is your partner's? We looked at whether opposites really attract, and what the best formula is for a happy couple. You used a questionnaire to identify your personality type and discussed your profile.

[Week 8] Be Grateful For The Good: We looked at the world's most powerful habit, gratitude, and how gratitude makes us happier and healthier. You practiced a gratitude exercise and discussed how you experience gratitude.

[Week 9] Make A Care Package: You learned about the origins of CARE packages and made a care package for your partner. You discussed gift giving in your family, and how that has shaped your expectations and hopes around gifts and holidays now.

[Week 10] Treat Yourself: You learned about the benefits of savoring, and how positive emotions do more than just make us feel good. You treated yourself to something(s) you enjoy by designing a beautiful day out.

[Week 11] Give To Others: How does giving make us happier and healthier? You learned four surprising ways that giving is good for us and 22 good ways to give to others. You performed some random acts of kindness and discussed generosity.

YOUR TASK THIS WEEK

Your task this week is to look over the list of topics you've covered in this series (above) and pick one topic you'd like to "refresh" and "re-do." You can each review the same topic, or choose to focus on different topics.

After you've each selected your topic, re-read that chapter and then *do* something to extend your review.

Repeat the exercises you originally did, or do something else. You might want to do some extra reading on this topic, or dig more deeply. Here are a couple of examples of ways you could dig more deeply on specific topics.

Example 1: Love Languages

If you decide to focus on love languages you could do some or all of the following:

- Review your primary love languages, and your partner's.
- Brainstorm a list of ways you could speak your partner's love language, then do something from your list.
- Read the love languages book by Gary Chapman, browse around the love languages website, or find some articles on love languages to read online.
- Ask your Facebook friends or Instagram community who has heard about the love languages framework and what their primary love languages are.

Example 2: Strengths

If you'd like to focus on strengths you could do some or all of the following:

- Review your signature strengths, and your partner's.
- Read some more about strengths. Browse around the *VIA Institute On Character* website. Or visit the *Authentic Happiness* website.
- Take the longer version of the VIA Signature Strengths test on the Authentic Happiness site (also free, 240 questions) and see how your results compare to the shorter version used on the VIA Institute website.
- Practice using one of your signature strengths in a new way this week.

Those are just two examples of how you could expand your learning on a particular topic. Pick the week that most interested you, and learn something extra on that topic.

DURING YOUR DATE

During your date this week, take some time to look back over this series together. Here are some questions to get you started, with space to make some notes about your thoughts in advance:

1. What has doing this series been like for you?

____

____

____

____

____

2. What were the topics you enjoyed the most?

____

____

____

____

____

3. What topics did you enjoy the least?

____

____

____

____

____

4. What is something new you've learned about yourself during this series?

____

____

____

____

____

5. What is something new you've learned about your partner during this series?

____

____

____

____

____

6. What topic did you decide to dig deeper in this week? Why?

____

____

____

____

____

7. What did you to do review, refresh, and practice that topic this week?

____

____

____

____

____

8. What is something you'd still like to learn more about?

____

____

____

____

____

9. What is something you will "take away" from this series—something you will do differently in the future?

____

____

____

____

____

CONGRATULTIONS

Congratulations on completing this entire series. Well done!!

Thanks for coming with me on this Deeper Dates journey. I feel honored that you chose to spend some of your precious time this way, and I hope this series sparked some great, thought-provoking discussions. I hope that you know yourself and your partner better now than you did three months ago. And I hope you had fun along the way.

What's next for you now? If you're looking for more activities and resources, check out www.coupleconnectors.com.

And if you're in a long distance relationship you can find more advice and activities just for you at www.modernlovelongdistance.com.

If you have any feedback or questions or anything else I can help you with, I'd love to hear from you.

Drop me a line anytime at lisa@coupleconnectors.com.

Thanks again. I'm wishing you all the best as you continue to learn more about each other and yourself, and as you continue on in these adventurous journeys we call life and love.

All my best,

Lisa

REFERENCES

[1] Peterson, T. D. & Peterson, E. W. (2008). *Stemming the tide of law student depression: What law schools need to learn from the science of positive psychology.* Yale Journal of Health Policy, Law, and Ethics, 9 (2).

[2] Learn more at: http://www.viacharacter.org/www/Character-Strengths-Survey.

[3] Learn more at: http://www.5lovelanguages.com/gary-chapman/

[4]As described by TIME Magazine in their series on Health and Happiness. Learn more at: http://content.time.com/time/specials/2007/article/0,28804,1631176_1630611_1630586,00.html

[5] Parker-Pope, T. (2010). *The Science Of A Happy Marriage.* Published by the New York Times. Learn more at: https://well.blogs.nytimes.com/2010/05/10/tracking-the-science-of-commitment/.

[6] Learn more at: https://www.theatlantic.com/national/archive/2013/07/more-evidence-reading-good-you/313575/

[7] As cited in *6 Science-Backed Reasons To Read Right Now:* http://www.huffingtonpost.com/2015/08/05/health-benefits-reading_n_4081258.html

[8] Baumeister, R.F. et al. (2001) *The Bad Is Stronger Than The Good,* Review Of General Psychology (5,4) 323-370.

9 *In Praise Of Gratitude.* A Harvard Mental Health Letter. Learn more at: https://www.health.harvard.edu/newsletter_article/in-praise-of-gratitude. And *7 Scientifically Proven Benefits Of Gratitude That Will Motivate You To Give Thanks Year-Round*, by Amy Morin (2014) in Forbes Magazine. Learn more at: https://www.forbes.com/sites/amymorin/2014/11/23/7-scientifically-proven-benefits-of-gratitude-that-will-motivate-you-to-give-thanks-year-round/

---

[10] Emmons, R. A. & McCullough, M. E. (2003). *Counting blessings versus burdens: An experimental investigation of gratitude and subjective well-being in daily life.* Journal of Personality and Social Psychology, 84, 377-389.

[11] Seligman, M. (2011) *Flourish: A Visionary New Understanding Of Happiness And Well Being.* Simon & Schuster.

[12] For more on this, see Martin Seligman's book *Flourish,* pages 80 and 140.

[13] Learn more at: https://positivepsychologyprogram.com/broaden-build-theory/

[14] See, for example: *The Paradox of Generosity: Giving We Receive, Grasping We Lose* by Christian Smith & Hilary Davidson (2014) Oxford University Press.

[15] Moll, J. et al (2006). *Human fronto–mesolimbic networks guide decisions about charitable donation.* PNAS (Vol 103, #42), 15623–15628.

[16] See Dunn, E. & Norton, M. (June 28, 2013), *How Money Actually Buys Happiness.* Harvard Business Review.

[17] S. Lyubomirsky, K. M. Sheldon, D. Schkade, *Rev. Gen. Psychol.* **9**, 111 (2005).

[18] See Oman, D. (2007). *Does volunteering foster physical health and longevity?* In S.G. Post (Ed.), Altruism and health: Perspectives from empirical research (pp. 15–32). New York: Oxford University Press.

[19] See Brown SL, Smith DM, Schulz R et al. (2009) *Caregiving behavior is associated with decreased mortality risk.* Psychol Sci. 2009;20(4):488–494.

[20] See Chan, A.L. (2013). *7 Science-Backed Reasons Why Generosity Is Good For Your Health.* Healthy Living, 12/01/2013.

[21] Lyubomirksy, S. (2007). *The How of Happiness: A New Approach to Getting the Life You Want.* Penguin Books.

[22] Seligman, M. (2011) *Flourish: A Visionary New Understanding Of Happiness And Well Being.* Simon & Schuster.

Made in the USA
San Bernardino, CA
18 April 2020

67941362R00061